The Car, The Sled, and The Butch Wax

Marc Maurer
Editor

Large Type Edition

A KERNEL BOOK
published by
NATIONAL FEDERATION OF THE BLIND

Copyright © 2003 by the
National Federation of the Blind

ISBN 1-885218-26-5

All Rights Reserved

Printed in the United States of America

Table of Contents

To Race with Blindness:
The Car and the College Student
by Marc Maurer 1

Butch Wax
by Susan Jones 16

The Day We All Went Sledding
by Allison Hilliker 21

Falling and Flying
by Sheila Koenig 32

Paying the Bill
by Peggy Elliott 39

On the Carrying of Trays and
the Use of Soda Machines
by Nathanael Wales 47

Cab 452
by Scott C. LaBarre 55

Diving
by Terri Uttermohlen 68

Editor's Introduction

For all of us, blind or sighted, there are crucial experiences which shape the way we look at ourselves—which help define who we are and what we are to become.

If we are fortunate, these experiences create within us a spirit of adventure, which leads us through the days of our lives with a sense of joy and anticipation. The particular happening or event that kindles the spirit matters little. It can be a car or a sled or even a jar of butch wax. Despite the apparent significance or the lack of it, they offer new perspective.

We who are blind have been sharing such experiences with you the readers of the Kernel Books for more than a dozen years, and we do so again in stories in this twenty-fourth volume in the series, *The Car, The Sled, and The Butch Wax.*

In these pages you will go scuba diving under the sea in the company of a blind woman vacationing in the Caribbean Islands, flying through the air with a blind teacher inspiring her students, and sledding in the snow with a blind student building her future. You will watch a young blind mechanic rebuild a Ford V8 engine and dream about cars that move out.

Through it all you continue to become more and more a part of the work of the National Federation of the Blind and help to bring new dimensions and possibilities to the lives of this generation of blind Americans.

We are now constructing the National Federation of the Blind Research and Training Institute, a five-story building at the National Center for the Blind in South

Marc Maurer, President
National Federation of the Blind

Baltimore. We will carry the spirit of adventure with us in the programs that we have already established and those that we initiate. We need people who understand us, and we know that you do. You contribute to this spirit of adventure that we prize so highly. You reflect and reinforce the belief that we who are blind are normal people with something to give to our friends and neighbors.

Some of the blind people we meet and inspire will be interested in mechanics. Some of us will find our hope and our joy in other fields. All of us will be encouraged by the respect you offer and the support you give. And I suspect some of us will want cars that move out.

Marc Maurer
Baltimore, Maryland
2003

WHY LARGE TYPE?

The type size used in this book is 14-point for two important reasons: One, because typesetting of 14-point or larger complies with federal standards for the printing of materials for visually impaired readers, and we want to show you what type size is helpful for people with limited sight.

The second reason is that many of our friends and supporters have asked us to print our paperback books in 14-point type so they too can easily read them. Many people with limited sight do not use Braille. We hope that by printing this book in a larger type than customary, many more people will be able to benefit from it.

To Race with Blindness: The Car and the College Student

by Marc Maurer

My son David loves cars. He comes by it honestly—I have always had a fascination for them myself. He is eighteen, and he thinks foreign cars are better than the American makes, but I like the American machines.

When David was about to become sixteen, he and his mom persuaded me to buy a car—a 1994 Chrysler New Yorker. My wife and I are both blind, and we had never before owned an automobile. I liked the big old New Yorker, but David thought it was an old man's car. He wanted a Volkswagen. In April of 2001 we bought a shiny new black Volkswagen GTI with a 1.8 turbo engine. I did not know how important it was to have a 1.8 turbo! David filled me in.

I have been blind all of my life, and my wife Patricia is also blind. Our children, David and Dianna, are both sighted. My wife and I have never been able to drive a car—except in a parking lot under supervision. Our children, on the other hand, believe that one of the roads to happiness involves the steering wheel.

David and I approach the subject of the automobile differently. He wants the car to look right. I want it to operate smoothly and efficiently. He wants the car to be the right color, to have the impressive nameplate, to be decorated with the appropriate stylish additions to the body, and to have the suspension lowered to within three or four inches of the ground. The Volkswagen he drives today is so low it would get stuck if it ran into the shadow of a fat telephone pole. I care less about the

Marc Maurer and his son David.

appearance of the machine than I do about the way it works, but both of us want the car to be able to move out.

David is finishing his freshman year at West Virginia University, 200 miles from Baltimore. Before he enrolled, we drove to West Virginia to visit the campus using the Volkswagen GTI with the 1.8 turbo. As we traveled west on Interstate-70, I noticed that the car was beginning to hum. I said to David, "I think that'll be enough." He responded, "Okay," and he took his foot off the gas. Later I asked him how fast we had been going. He told me that the car had been moving at something over a hundred miles per hour.

Today, I have a family, and we do things together. But there was a time when I wondered whether this could be so. Part of my progress in coming to realize that blindness is not an insuperable obstacle involved an automobile.

I grew up as a blind child, and I faced the assumptions of many who believed that blind people have little to contribute. I did not play basketball or baseball, and I was not able to handle pictures. However, I was interested in science and mechanics, and I did well in school. I took first place in a high school science contest for my explanation of the use and value of two-cycle and four-cycle gasoline engines. With these experiences, I hoped that I might be able to learn mechanics, and I wanted to get my hands on a car.

Many of my friends in high school had cars, and occasionally I helped fix them up. But it was only tinkering—I never learned enough to be good at it.

When I graduated from high school, I enrolled in a program to teach blind adults directed by Dr. Kenneth Jernigan, who was then the President of the National Federation of the Blind. Dr. Jernigan, who was himself blind, told me that blind people can do almost anything that sighted people can do using alternative skills for the blind.

Blind people are often urged to sit peacefully and wait. Dr. Jernigan demanded that we take action and move. The program included classes in physical education, home economics, Braille, communication using typewriters and other keyboard instruments, instruction in the way to use a white cane to travel safely and effectively, and woodshop. There was also a class in the proper approach to the subject of blindness. Because blindness is so frequently misunderstood, a positive philosophy must be created to teach blind students that it is the misunderstanding of blindness, not the blindness itself, that interferes with living an independent life.

Philosophy, of course, is all very well, but it takes a demonstration to drive home the point. Some people learn that blindness is not an insurmountable barrier in gym class. Some learn it traveling with a cane. Some discover this reality by cooking a meal for a dozen friends in home economics. I think I learned to appreciate this teaching in all of these ways, but I loved the shop best. For the first time I was able to put my hands on expensive wood- and metalworking tools. I could cut sheets of wood with precision or machine metal parts.

In shop class we went through a number of preliminary exercises to teach us how to handle the tools. When we had completed these, we were expected to select a substantial project to demonstrate that we had mastered the skills involved. Some blind people built tables, chairs, or beds. One man fashioned a ball-peen hammer out of steel. One man constructed a poker table with special slots for glasses and chips. It was octagonal with a felt top. Many years later I played cards at that table.

When it was my turn to select a project, the shop teacher asked me what I wanted to build. I told him I didn't want to build anything. "So, what do you want to do?" he asked me.

"I want to overhaul an automobile engine," I said.

"Do you have a car?" he wanted to know.

"No," I said.

"Can you get a car?" he wanted to know.

"Sure," I said. I had no idea where I would get a car. I was eighteen years old with no job and no money.

He said that he would look into the matter and let me know.

In one sense, I was testing the system. Many people had told me that I could do whatever I wanted to do. When I asked how I could do it, they responded by telling me that they would find out. Most of the time I did not hear from them again. The program Dr. Jernigan was directing seemed different from others. When he said blind people could do things, he frequently found ways to demonstrate that they could.

About a week after my conversation with the shop teacher, he came to me to say that we were going on a trip to the hardware store. We were going to buy the tools to overhaul an automobile engine.

When we got to the hardware store, my teacher asked me if I thought we would need some wrenches. I thought we would. He then wondered if we might require a toolbox in which to keep all the items. I thought we would need that. Didn't I think we would need a hoist? That also, it seemed to me, we would need. Then he asked me if we would need some pullers. I had never heard of a puller in my life.

"Oh, yes," I said. "We'll definitely need them."

Pretty soon we had several thousand dollars worth of equipment lying on the counter. I touched the wrenches and other tools with my fingers, and I thought to myself, "I better get a car."

I called one of my buddies from high school. I told him that I would like to borrow a car for a few months. I said that I would rebuild his engine for him, and he agreed. Soon there was a 1963 Ford Galaxy 500 parked out front with an 8-cylinder 352-cubic-inch engine in it.

Although we had purchased a hoist to lift the engine from the car, we had no place to hang it. So the first job was to build a beam to hold the weight of the hoist and anything it would lift. We did this by gluing and nailing together five two-by-twelves. We mounted these atop two six-by-eights that had been nailed to concrete pillars. During the process of nailing these boards to the pillars I became acquainted for the first time with a nail gun. A nail gun uses a 22-caliber rifle shell to shoot a nail into concrete. I had been wondering what we would do to drive the nails into the pillars. With a nail gun this is no problem at all.

With the hoist in place, we lifted the engine from the Ford. I had built a wooden engine stand to hold the piece of machinery. We pushed the car out of the way, and my teacher began to show me how rebuilding an engine is done. Before we had finished, I had every single piece of that 352-inch V-8 in my hands, and I learned a lot about car engines and also something about blindness.

Taking a complex piece of machinery apart, replacing worn elements, machining pieces that needed refurbishment, and reassembling the whole demand patience and organization. After an engine has been run for a while, the crankshaft may become worn. I tested its measurements with a micrometer, and I discovered that the crankshaft needed to be "turned." This means that the bearing surfaces needed machining so that they would all be the same size. When this has been done, oversized bearings are installed so that the engine will run smoothly and without vibration. In addition, I installed oversized piston rings and reseated the valves. We even considered installing a racing camshaft, but this would have demanded boring out the cylinders, changing the crankshaft, and procuring new racing heads. I didn't have the money for that, but the idea was nice.

Some people think that if you want to play a trick on your mechanic you should take two or three pieces of the mechanism and hide them. This is not the best way. If you remove essential parts, the mechanic will notice and look for them. If you add pieces that don't really belong but appear to have some useful purpose, the mechanic will spend time being mystified about where they go.

I'm not certain that my friends were playing a trick upon me. However, when I got the engine back together there were two or three parts leftover that didn't seem to be needed for anything. I have always wondered who put these into the parts box.

Fortunately, when the engine had been reassembled and hoisted back into the engine compartment, it kicked over at the first turn of the starter and purred as a well-built 352 should. I had the satisfaction of experiencing firsthand the notion that blindness cannot prevent a human being from becoming a successful mechanic. If this is true, I thought, how much else can be accomplished?

A number of years later at a convention of the National Federation of the Blind, I met a blind person who was then serving as the chief mechanic for the American Automobile Club. By that time I had enrolled at the University of Notre Dame, and I had decided that my career would probably not involve repairing automobile engines.

Later still I was invited to spend a day in Indianapolis, Indiana, during the Indianapolis 500. A blind man was assisting with computer telemetry for the Dick Simon racing team, and I observed the race from the perspective of one of the groups that put a car on the track. I was not a blind mechanic, but I did help a blind person who was assisting the mechanics to ensure that the car being driven at the Indianapolis Speedway operated within the tolerances they had established.

The spirit of adventure that involved the rebuilding of a Ford V-8 has been with me ever since. The planning for tomorrow, the creation of innovative programs to enhance opportunity, and the development of new techniques to achieve success in unusual fields are all part of the National Federation of the Blind.

Those of us who are blind will not be in the driver's seat with our hands on the wheel, but some of us will develop the talent to build the cars. Our world is filled with competition, and we know that with proper training and belief in ourselves—with a dream in our heart and the support of our friends—we can compete along with our sighted neighbors. Beyond that, we must find ways to help others learn the same thing. It is of vital importance that we teach our children to know that they also have something to contribute.

This is what we have learned in the National Federation of the Blind, and this is what we are passing on to those we meet. I suspect that an essential ingredient (at least for me) is that some of us want cars that will move out.

BUTCH WAX

by Susan Jones

Susan Jones lives in Indianapolis and is a leader in the National Federation of the Blind of Indiana. Much of our work in the Federation revolves around striving for various kinds of "equality" in our lives. Reporting a delightfully humorous incident from her own childhood, Susan points out that blind youngsters sometimes have no problem in achieving equality of mischievousness. Here is what she has to say:

I was born blind in 1951, the second of five children, the rest all being sighted. One morning, when I was about five, my older brother Doug entered the kitchen for breakfast, and my mother said, "Your hair's

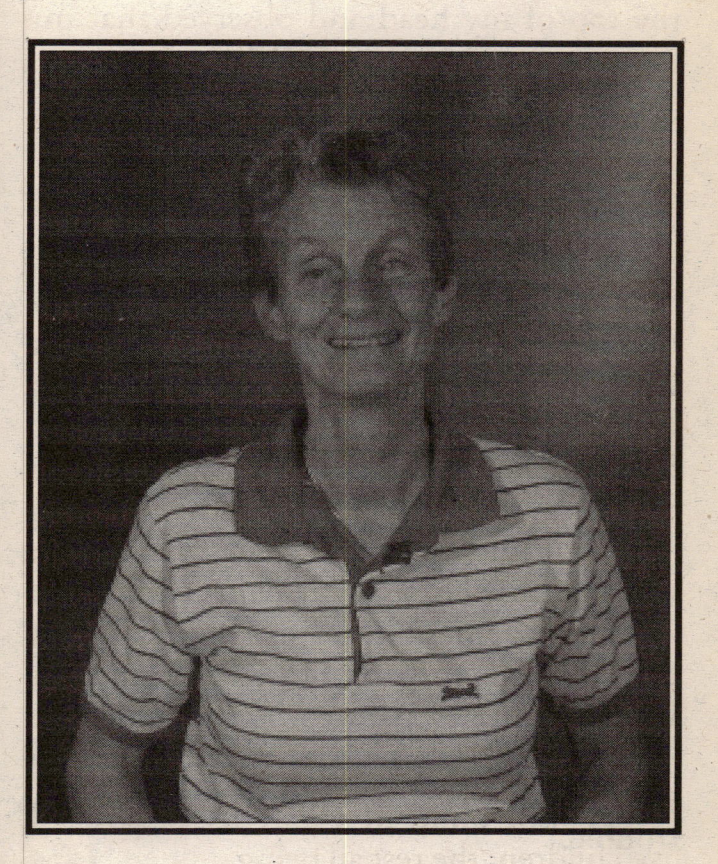

Susan Jones

standing straight up!" I put my hands to the top of my head and observed that my hair was lying down, quite flat.

"How does he do that, Mom?" I asked.

"Butch Wax," she said.

Now, for some reason, I thought I would really look neat with my hair standing straight on end. So, as I finished my breakfast and went out to play, I plotted to find that Butch Wax.

Lunchtime came and went, and soon it was naptime. I used to nap in my older brother's room. I heard my mother as she gave her parting remarks to Madonna Blessing, our new nanny who had just come: "I'm going to the club to swim. The kids are in bed. They shouldn't give you any trouble."

I heard the car drive out. "Good," I thought, "I've got some time to look for this stuff." I went to Doug's dresser and, soon enough, found a small jar. I opened it up and sniffed—yes, this must be it. Now, how much would it take? I reached three fingers in and grabbed a bunch, applying it liberally to my long hair. It smelled and felt so luxurious as I worked it into my tresses.

I will never know what made Madonna come up and check on me, but I heard footsteps, so I rushed to close and replace the little jar. The door opened suddenly. "Susan, what are you doing?" she gasped.

She shampooed my hair with hot water, then again with cold water; but nothing took out the Butch Wax. She was sure my mother would be horrified when she returned home. She was right. Mom and her friend Mrs. Toney, who lived next door, spent all evening trying to remove the greasy stuff. They pulled with paper towels, then toilet paper.

Finally, after supper, Mrs. Toney said, "Why don't you try Cheer." Cheer was what we washed our laundry with. So, my mother laid me on the top of the freezer, dangling my head into the washtub. She soaped my hair with Cheer and rinsed it out. Sure enough, most of the wax was removed. The rest would take days, perhaps weeks, to wear out.

What does this story have to do with my being blind? Well, nothing really, except to show that blind kids, like sighted kids, are curious and like to try things out. Happily, most of us, and our gray-haired parents, live to tell about it decades later.

We in the National Federation of the Blind believe that the average blind kid can get into the average amount of trouble in childhood in the average amount of time, as well as or better than the average sighted kid. How else can we be prepared to compete on terms of equality with our sighted peers?

THE DAY WE ALL WENT SLEDDING

by Allison Hilliker

Allison Hilliker is a thoughtful young woman with a passion to become a teacher. Teachers frequently have to be prepared to deal with the unexpected. In The Day We All Went Sledding, *Allison shows that she'll be up to the task. Here is what she has to say:*

Can a blind person be a teacher? I mean, could I, as a blind woman, really be expected to run a classroom? A situation such as that would involve monitoring the activities of children, organizing a learning environment, dealing with mountains of printed materials, effectively communicating

Allison Hilliker

academic concepts to my students, and my generally being responsible for every bit of learning done by more than two dozen kids.

Sounds like a daunting task for a college student to undertake, but that's what I've decided I want to do. Education and work with children is my passion, and I am willing to find ways to make it happen. There are many different techniques that a blind teacher can use in order to run a classroom, and most of them I have been fortunate enough to learn through my experiences with educators in the National Federation of the Blind.

Thus far, things have gone well for me as I take my first steps into the field of teaching, but there was one Thursday afternoon in mid February, that would challenge everything I had in the way of philosophy and confidence. That was the day that we all went sledding.

I am just beginning to study elementary education. With my first education class, Educational Psychology, I have what is known as a field placement. This means that I get to be in an actual classroom at least once a week. I have second grade, and it's gone well so far. The teacher and all of the students are sighted, so I have to do a great deal of proving myself as a competent blind person, capable of working in a classroom.

Every day is an adventure, but so far things have been going well. The kids see me as a teacher-like figure, and the classroom teacher has been giving me ever-increasing levels of responsibility. It's true that we all have been able to learn a great deal from one another.

I typically visit the class on Thursday mornings, but this particular week saw me having an afternoon visit. The classroom teacher forgot that I was coming on this day, and that very afternoon turned out to be a special sledding time for the kids. When I walked in to the class, the teacher said something to the effect of, "Oh no, I forgot that you were coming. We're sledding today, and can you do that?" Those really were not the words I had been expecting to hear, but I just smiled and said, "Certainly, I can sled—not a problem." I was really thinking, "Oh boy. Here goes!"

Now, having grown up in the Midwest, I had been sledding a number of times. I knew that it was something I could do well as a blind person, but I also realized that the others didn't necessarily know this. I was fully aware of the possible problems associated with my sledding with twenty some of these kids. I was fairly certain that most of them and their teacher did not believe that sledding was something I could do safely.

Sure enough, without asking me about what I thought, the teacher announced to the class that, before heading outside, they would all sit in a circle while I explained to them how best they could help me while we were sledding. I was surprised at this idea because the teacher had never specifically asked the kids to do anything for me before.

I wasn't exactly certain that I liked this new turn of events. If the kids felt as though they had to take care of me, how could they also be expected to view me as a teacher? I wanted to tell her that there really wasn't anything specific that anyone need do, but she had already made the announcement to the class, and I didn't want to make it a bigger issue than it already was. So, we gathered around, and I took the chance to re-explain my cane and what it does. This gave me the chance to reaffirm that I did not in fact need help, while still complying with what the classroom teacher had asked me to do.

I also reassured, more for the teacher's benefit rather than the kids', that I could do a lot by sound and that I would hear an approaching sled and move out of the way if I had to. I tried to make everything seem as normal and as easy as possible. The kids were fine with this, so we headed out.

Again without asking me first, the teacher next tried to assign one of the kids to guide me around outside. I was getting a bit frustrated by this point, but I knew that I could not let it show. The intentions of the teacher and the student were good, and I had to remember that. I don't mind accepting help when it's necessary, but I also wanted the class to view me as a competent person and knew that letting a child guide me around wouldn't be in keeping with that image.

If I start letting others do too much for me, I can't expect anyone to respect me when I go to try to obtain a job teaching. I knew that I had the skills to be successful in the sledding activity and believed it important that I had the opportunity to demonstrate them.

So I politely explained to both the child and the teacher that a guide wouldn't be necessary. I would be able to manage. The explanation seemed to suffice, and I headed towards the hill, using my cane and following the sounds of talking and laughing children.

Well, the hill on the playground was pretty chaotic, even if it was only the one class out at that time. All I can say is, thank goodness for the blindness skills I've obtained; otherwise I would likely never have managed. There were kids, sleds, snow, and ice everywhere. Sighted or blind, the hill was crazy and alive with child activity. I took a deep breath, gathered myself, and carrying my sled and my cane, made my way up to the top of that hill.

When it was all said and done, I thought it had gone rather well. I discovered that it was really an enjoyable experience to sled with the kids. We eventually played and laughed so hard that blindness just was no longer an issue.

There were a few instances where someone was hesitant to have me climb the hill by myself, but after a while of their seeing that I could do it, they forgot and became used to it. I sledded down that hill with the kids, and things went smoothly. The classroom teacher was sledding too, by the way, so my sledding with the kids was only what was expected of everyone.

The best part of the experience was when a couple of the girls in the class even begged me to race down the hill with them. This was something that made me feel completely accepted. When it was all over, I was tired, cold, and sore but happy that things had gone well.

Not one person offered to guide me on the way back into the school, so I felt that I had done some educating. I helped the kids gather their sleds, and we walked into the school together. I like to think that everyone, kids and teacher, learned a little bit on that afternoon.

The day's sledding adventure seems like such a small thing in some ways, but we as blind people know that it wasn't the least bit small. In fact, it was an accomplishment for us all. I think that, as a blind student, I often get very tired of having to prove myself to people all the time, but on days like this one, when it seems to work, when I actually see the difference, it's so worthwhile.

When we are challenged to do things that we are uncertain about, when our philosophy must be put into practice, and when we are able to educate even a small group of people while doing so, then it's a victory for us all.

That's what we all are working to do in the National Federation of the Blind. Each individual in our organization can help our cause through his or her own small victories.

Every job we get, every class we pass, and every hill we sled down is a piece in a larger process. The NFB is filled with committed persons who believe that the blind can be normal, successful, happy, and contributing members of society. It is through this organization that I have gained the confidence I need to pursue my dreams of teaching. The members of the NFB are people who demonstrate, through their everyday experiences, that blind people can work, play, teach, and even sled, along with the sighted.

Falling and Flying

by Sheila Koenig

In 1995 Sheila Koenig won a scholarship from the National Federation of the Blind. Later she became a student at one of our training centers. Today she is an inspiring and dedicated middle-school English teacher. Along the way she learned to confront a paralyzing fear of falling. Here is how she tells her story:

Every summer during my childhood my family ventured out on at least one camping trip. My brother David and I conjured up fantastic adventures wherever we went. Building enchanted hideouts or mystical sand sculptures, we embarked as pioneers to chart new territory. Though blind since birth, I have not always traveled with a long

Sheila Koenig

white cane; during the expeditions with my brother I squinted at the ground in front of me and let him lead, even though he was younger.

I anticipated our adventures with enthusiastic curiosity, eager to unleash my imagination in each magnificent place we discovered. But straining and squinting became tiresome, and my incompetence at times created in me genuine apprehension to explore rocky or unfamiliar terrain.

The summer we camped at Devil's Lake in Baraboo, Wisconsin, I realized the magnitude of my ineffective travel technique. Hiking along the bluffs, which rose nearly five hundred feet, I clenched my father's hand. He tried his best to guide me along the trails, but I clung to him, paralyzed with the fear of falling. I understood that trusting my residual vision compromised my abilities, but I knew no alternative techniques. As I gathered the courage to finish the hike, I promised myself that someday I would not allow my blindness to thwart my ambitions.

Years later I stood atop a different bluff, one that I had climbed while wearing sleep shades as a student at Blindness: Learning in New Dimensions (BLIND), one of our Federation training centers. Upon graduating from high school, I had won a scholarship from the National Federation of the Blind, and part of the scholarship included attending the national convention.

At national conventions I observed blind people traveling confidently with the long white cane. I realized that, if I had learned Braille, I would not be holding large-print books close to my face in an awkward attempt to read them.

Since those childhood days of expeditions with my brother, I had aspired to be a teacher. But questions always lurked beneath the surface of my dream: How would I read the class attendance roll? How would I grade papers and complete lesson plans? How would I approach the topic of blindness with my students? With the help of the National Federation of the Blind, I observed that alternative techniques existed, and I recognized that, before I could become a successful teacher, I must first acquire the skills to become a successful blind person.

I developed these skills at BLIND. Daily lessons in travel, Braille, and computers built my competence, but one activity more than any other launched my confidence. My initial reaction to rock climbing was one of anxiety and fear.

I speculated that falling would probably not be any less frightening if I were attached to climbing gear. But as I listened to other blind people clamoring with excitement, I became more eager to climb. When I touched the anchor at the top after my first climb, I smiled with proud exhilaration, confidence rushing through my veins.

On the first day of school I challenged my ninth grade English students to stretch their imaginations, to explore the possibilities of language and images in the world around them, and to confront the fears that paralyze them. Showing students the way, however, does a better job of inspiring than simply telling them.

I began my presentation this year with a video recorded two weeks prior to the start of school; I had ridden the Skycoaster at the Minnesota State Fair. Tightly secured in our harnesses, Jennifer Dunnam and I ascended a 150-foot tower. Upon reaching our perch at the top, she pulled the cord, sending us plummeting towards the ground. I screamed through the initial fall, but as we began to glide back and forth, pendulum style, I marveled at the exhilaration of flying.

My students also marveled at seeing their English teacher falling through the air and flying triumphantly. They too began to understand how to stretch the possibilities of their imaginations and dive into new experiences. I thrive on challenges and high expectations, but without the influence of the National Federation of the Blind, I would never have evolved beyond that fearful young girl clinging to others for guidance and direction.

PAYING THE BILL

by Peggy Elliott

Peggy Elliott lives and works in Grinnell, Iowa. Her sprightly stories have appeared in many previous Kernel Books. Here she looks back on an experience she had at the beginning of her adulthood. Her thoughtful reflection is tempered by years of experience as a successful attorney and active leader in the National Federation of the Blind.

I've been blind for most of my life, and I was blind when I earned my law degree and got my first job. I joked back then that I wanted a job, an apartment, and a cat in that order, and I followed the plan.

My very first apartment was the top floor of a large old house with a living room, dining room, and three bedrooms. It was roomy and had lots of windows for ventilation and for the cat to use to observe the world. His favorite window was the one that overlooked the sidewalk on which I returned home each night and, in the summer, he would sit in the open window and yell at me as I walked up to the house, demanding that I hurry up and get inside.

Then the first Iowa winter came on. As a blind apartment dweller, I had used a steel file to mark little notches in the thermostat so I could control the heat. Thinking ahead, I told myself. Or, I told myself that until the first heating bill arrived.

I panicked. It was huge! I couldn't pay that bill on my meager salary as an assistant county attorney. Especially since the next one would be as big! I called the landlord and insisted that he check the thermostat. It was fine. I called the power company

Doug and Peggy Elliott

and insisted that it double-check its reading and billing. It confirmed the figures as correct. I settled down to pay and close off rooms for the winter and add electric baseboard heating in the bedroom and learn all the little tricks of saving on one's energy bill.

But I always suspected that my encounter with the heat bill had something to do with my being blind. I couldn't see the thermostat; I couldn't read the bills myself; I didn't know things that sighted people did, and so the huge bill was self-inflicted because I was blind.

Readers may think this is illogical, but I'm only telling you what I thought at the time. I and many other blind people fall into the trap of attributing to blindness all the ills of our lives, and, rationally examined, the attributions don't hold up. That doesn't make them any less real to the blind person feeling inadequate about something.

My life moved on from the heating bill crisis. I've paid a lot of heat bills in my years living in Iowa. I got married, and my husband and I bought some residential rental property in our community as part of our investment strategy for the future. We now pay heating bills for some renters, and we have bought four new furnaces and fixed a lot more than that.

Last year, we rented a nice top floor apartment we own with lots of windows and a living room and a dining room and several bedrooms to a nice young woman who is sighted and who was moving out of her parents' home for the first time to take a job as a teacher.

When the first heating bills came out at the beginning of winter, we got a call from the frantic tenant. She asked us to come and check the thermostat since she had just gotten her first bill showing heating costs, and it was impossible that the cost was that gigantic. I heard later that she had also called the power company to ask them to do a re-reading on her bill because it had to be erroneous. Both the thermostat and the power company's readings were accurate just as they had been in my case.

I thought back to my own first apartment and to the feelings of inadequacy I had experienced at the onset of my first heating bill. I remembered with a mixture of amusement and sadness how much those feelings were based on my feeling inferior to sighted persons because I am blind.

I now know that the heating bill crisis is merely a rite of passage for all first-time renters or owners in cold climes. The sadness was for all my colleagues who are blind and who, like me, sometimes attribute to blindness what are normal human reactions to growing up or learning new skills or being the new person in a group of friends or work colleagues.

We blind people, like everyone else, are challenged to learn new things and succeed in trying circumstances and make friends in new settings. We, and sometimes those around us as well, can perceive difficulties in achieving these goals as stemming from our blindness when a sighted person in exactly the same situation would have exactly the same problem.

Through the National Federation of the Blind and my friendship with capable, competent blind people, I have learned to put my blindness in perspective. I no longer think that everything that goes wrong or is uncomfortable for me is automatically related to my blindness.

Some of it is, like the effort to find my first job when I applied to fifty law firms and was turned down by all fifty. My friends in the Federation encouraged me to keep trying, to believe in myself, to keep applying. I did, and I found that first job and that first apartment.

My friends in the National Federation of the Blind have taught me that it is my job to figure things out, to take responsibility, to take charge of my life. I've tried to do that since it makes sense to me, and I have forged the tools, as have my sighted colleagues, to find jobs, to pay those taxes, and to participate in my community's life. And, by the way, I just paid another heating bill.

On the Carrying of Trays and the Use of Soda Machines

by Nathanael Wales

Nathanael Wales is a blind college student at the University of California at Davis. He is fortunate that he found the National Federation of the Blind early on and has had the opportunity to receive good training. He takes his blindness in stride and does what he can to help others understand blindness. Here is what he has to say:

On June 6, 1996, I graduated from high school in Apple Valley, California. Nine days later I traveled to the Louisiana Center for the Blind in Ruston, Louisiana, to attend one of the National Federation of the Blind's training centers for blind children and adults.

While there I learned many alternative techniques for living productively and successfully as a blind person. These skills included reading and writing Braille, traveling with a long white cane, using a computer with a speech synthesizer and screen-reading software, and managing an apartment. My fellow students and I also did extracurricular activities to build our confidence as blind people and just have fun, including bowling, going to movies, white-water rafting, rock climbing, and being a part of Mardi Gras in New Orleans.

One of the many techniques for living successfully as a blind person that I learned (but at the time didn't believe I would use on a daily basis) was how to carry a tray at a fast-food restaurant or in a cafeteria. The technique is fairly simple once one knows how to do it.

Nathanael Wales

A blind person can take one arm, slide it under (and in some rare instances, over) the tray, grip the far side of the tray with the hand, and place the fingers against the cup or glass with the drink. The closer side of the tray can be rested against the waist and elbow. With the other hand, the long white cane can be used just as it would be if the blind diner were not carrying a tray at all.

My cane travel class began with the relatively small and lightweight trays at the McDonald's three blocks away from the Center, which happened to be a popular lunchtime restaurant for the students and staff. We visited a number of other restaurants, working our way up to Morrison's, a large cafeteria in Monroe with large, heavy trays; large, heavy dishes; tall, very full glasses; and very good food.

After I graduated from the Louisiana Center for the Blind I entered the University of California at Davis. I lived in the dorms for about a year and a half. I consequently ate in the dormitory cafeteria, the Dining Commons, and on a daily basis carried large trays with plates, bowls, and glasses.

I must also confess that I am addicted to Diet Coke, and to satisfy my addiction I learned to use the fountain soda machine. I found it was not at all hard to use: I just remembered which machine it was and where the button for Diet Coke was located. If I ever forgot, I'd just ask another student. By sticking a finger just below the rim of the glass I would know when the glass was full and would stop pressing the button on the machine.

The Dining Commons is, however, not the only place to eat on the campus of my university. There is the Silo, a food court with overpriced and not-too-good fast food. There is also the Coffee House, which is run by the Student Union. It's very inexpensive and has outstanding food and a diversity of it: sandwiches, an Asian bar, a Tex Mex Grill, pizza, and, of course, the bakery.

Students as well as non-students regularly meet friends at the Coffee House for lunch, and I frequently do the same with classmates, students from my church's campus fellowship, and other friends.

One particular noon I was meeting a good friend of mine from my campus fellowship at the Coffee House. He and I often eat lunch and hang out there. We talk about all sorts of things: school, hunting and fishing (he's an avid hunter and fisherman), sports, and spiritual things.

I've also talked about how I do things as a blind person and the attitude that I have developed through God's blessing me by providing for me to find and experience what the National Federation of the Blind and its leaders have given me. He's comfortable talking about my blindness, and we often talk about my work as a leader in the Federation.

On that particular noon we were holding our small cardboard trays, waiting for our orders from the Tex Mex Grill (they have excellent quesadillas). While we were waiting we went to get drinks from the fountain drink machines: he for ice water and I for Diet Coke. After I got my Diet Coke I stepped away from the machine to wait for my friend. As I stood there with my long white cane, my tray, and my full cup of soda, a girl walked up to me and asked if I needed help with the soda machine. I looked down at my full cup of Diet Coke a bit perplexed and said, "Uh, no. Thanks."

She left, and when my friend came back, I said, "You know, the most interesting thing just happened. As I was standing here waiting for you a girl came up to me and asked if I needed help with the soda machine."

I hope the fact that I was carrying my tray and using the soda machine successfully as a blind person might have changed the genuinely helpful girl's preconceived ideas about the abilities of blind people. But my friend laughed quietly with me, so I know that even if I haven't changed the girl's perceptions, I've accomplished something important.

Cab 452

by Scott C. LaBarre

Scott LaBarre is President of the National Federation of the Blind's special interest division for blind lawyers. There are elements of humor and irony in his story, which illustrates the profound disconnect that, all too often, still exists between the reality of blindness and the perception of it. Here is what Scott has to say about Cab 452:

I am a blind lawyer who owns and runs his own firm. Recently I got married, and my wife and I are proudly expecting our first child. We also look with joy towards living in a home that we just purchased. In other words, I normally think of myself as the

Scott C. LaBarre

typical young professional starting a family and pursuing a career.

From time to time, however, something occurs that reminds me that my blindness makes me vastly different from the average young American professional. Even though I have accomplished much in my life, sometimes people are not able to look past the fact that a blind man is before them, and when they concentrate so heavily on my blindness, their natural tendency is to prescribe to me the characteristics that they believe a blind person possesses rather than consider the life I have actually lived.

About a year ago, I elected to take a cab home from the office for the specific reason of swinging by the drycleaner to collect a bunch of clothes I had dropped off the previous day. I needed to collect the clothes because the next day I was flying off on a business trip in connection with one of my cases.

After waiting outside of my office building for a short while, Metro Taxi's Cab 452 came speeding up. Soon after getting in the cab, I immediately realized that the driver was in a hurry because he rapidly flew out of the parking lot. When I told him that I had to make a stop at the drycleaner, the driver groaned. Upon later reflection, I am certain that I unconsciously adopted this guy's impatience. So as we rocketed up to the drycleaner, my desire was to make the retrieval of my clothes as expeditious as possible.

When he said "We're here," I quickly opened the door and heard a sickening "thunk" noise. This driver had parked his size 12 cab into a size 10 parking space. You guessed it. I opened my door onto someone else's vehicle.

As I wriggled myself out of the cab, I heard somebody running up and screaming "You, (expletive deleted), scratched my new SUV!" As soon as this new SUV owner realized that

I was blind, he immediately turned his wrath upon the cab driver. Then began an hour-long ordeal.

My cab driver's first tongue was not English, and the SUV owner's use of the language was grotesque, to put it kindly. SUV Man screamed at the driver, "How the (expletive deleted) can you park so close to my car and let the blind man out there?" Mr. Cab Driver yelled back, claiming that there was no scratch and that it was not a big deal. He also said, "Give this poor blind guy a break. He couldn't see your stupid car."

SUV Man kept yelling at Mr. Cab Driver that he better damn well pay for the repairs. Mr. Cab Driver said, "There is no damage. We're leaving!" SUV Man replied, "There is no (expletive deleted) way you're leaving. I'm calling the police!"

From there, the conversation degenerated quickly between these gentlemen while they hurled vicious insults back and forth. They both went into the drycleaner to accost potential eyewitnesses about what happened. I followed the quarrelling twosome into the store and attempted to gain their attention. No one was paying me any mind amidst the raging storm of verbal putdowns.

We in the National Federation of the Blind often say that we seek to achieve first-class citizenship for the nation's blind. We also say that with such first-class citizenship comes first-class responsibility. At the time this event occurred, I remember feeling at fault for what happened. I told myself, "You should have been more cautious and opened the door more slowly."

I also asked myself what would have happened if I were a sighted man getting out of the cab? I suspect that the sighted man would bear the responsibility for what transpired as a result of his lack of caution.

On that day, I attempted to get the attention of the two men so that I could discuss with them my role in the whole mess. At first, they were ignoring me altogether. Finally, I stepped in front of SUV Man and handed him my business card.

As I started to say something to him about the fact the he could call me about any potential damages, he said, "You don't have to give me your lawyer's card. You're blind. It's not your fault." Handing the card back to me, he once again said, "I don't need to talk with your lawyer. This stupid cab driver will need a lawyer." Then the cab driver chimed in, "It isn't this blind man's fault. Give the poor guy a break. And I am not the stupid one."

I then tried to tell both gentlemen that I was, in fact, a lawyer and that my purpose was to help resolve the dispute. Once again, they ignored me and took their battle outside of the store.

Later, the police did, in fact, arrive. The officer examined SUV Man's vehicle and said that he could see no scratch. The officer spoke with both gentlemen, and they both described me as "this poor blind guy." The officer agreed that whatever had happened was "not the blind guy's fault." The officer never once spoke with me to ask about what had happened.

Finally, the ordeal came to an end with both combatants yelling at each other and getting in a few last insults. On the way home, I attempted to tell the driver of Cab 452 that I felt bad about what happened. After all, I opened the door onto SUV Man's prized possession. The cab driver stated over and over that "Life must be hard man. It isn't your fault." I repeatedly tried to explain that my life was fine.

When we got to my home, I left the cab telling him that his supervisor could call me at my law office if there were any lingering questions. Apparently, no official action resulted from the incident because I never heard from anyone regarding the matter.

Several weeks after the event, Cab 452 once again answered my call for a taxi and again picked me up from my office. The guy immediately said that he was the driver who had taken me to the drycleaner, and he launched into an account of how stupid and ugly SUV Man had been. Then he asked me, "Is that building your doctor's or counselor's office?" I said "no" and explained that I was a lawyer and that the building was home to my office.

The driver of Cab 452 was shocked. He asked me, "You work? Work as a lawyer?" I again told him what I did for a living, and he repeatedly commented that he was impressed and couldn't believe it.

The incident at the drycleaner and the subsequent ride in Cab 452 are not earthshattering events but are the kinds of events that remind me that I am not the average young professional chasing the American dream. Such events force me to reflect upon the status of blind people in our society.

At the drycleaner, initially, SUV Man started yelling at me about the alleged damage done to his car. Once he saw my white cane and realized that I was blind, all blame instantaneously shifted to the cab driver. Both at that time and afterwards, the driver made comments that said, in effect, "Give the poor blind guy a break."

Does my blindness absolve me of all responsibility in this kind of affair? Arguably, the cab driver probably should not have parked so close to another vehicle. However, maybe I shouldn't have been in such a hurry. Maybe I should have opened the door more slowly and carefully. Certainly SUV Man should not have overreacted and screamed so viciously and made a federal case out of such a small matter.

Regardless of how much blame should be assigned to the different individuals, there is no question in my mind that at least part of this accident was directly attributable to me and my actions. Neither the cab driver nor SUV Man nor the police officer ever wanted to hold me responsible in any way. They all agreed that I was faultless because of my blindness.

What struck me even more forcefully is how these gentlemen reacted to the fact that I am a lawyer. Their response was disbelief. When I handed SUV Man my card, he assumed that the card was somebody else's. He did not consider for a moment that I was the lawyer named on the card. The cab driver did not understand until much later that I was a lawyer with my own practice, even though I had explained it several times. When he finally understood that I practiced law, he was shocked, to say the least.

Blind people have served as lawyers in our country for decades. In fact, the first

President of the National Federation of the Blind, Dr. Jacobus tenBroek, practiced law and taught at a major university starting in the 1930s. Even though there have been many blind lawyers, the gentlemen involved in this incident either could not or would not believe that I, a blind man, was a lawyer.

This phenomenon occurs with quite some frequency as I travel through life. Not a month goes by without someone expressing their absolute surprise that I am employed as an attorney.

When I became blind as a ten-year-old boy, I literally thought that my life was over. In my wildest dreams, I never imagined that I could pursue a challenging career, marry a beautiful woman, raise a family, and own a home, but I am doing all those things. The National Federation of the Blind has taught me to believe in myself as a blind person. The Federation has also made me realize that we have an obligation to spread a positive philosophy about blindness and to educate society about the true abilities of the blind.

Incidentally, I saw Cab 452's driver recently. His name is Mustafa, and he now has a much broader understanding of how blind people get along in the world. After seeing and listening to me enough times, he has learned that blind persons function in all walks of life and do so well. He is no longer shocked that I am a lawyer, and my blindness does not seem to be something so unusual to him or something that should be pitied.

Our road to first-class citizenship has been long and hard, but we are getting there. Person by person, action by action, we change what it means to be blind. Cab 452 has reaffirmed my conviction that we will realize a day when the blind are full, first-class citizens in our society. With the work of the National Federation of the Blind and a society willing to listen, that day may not be all that far away.

DIVING

by Terri Uttermohlen

When Terri Uttermohlen considered the possibility of fulfilling her long-held dream of diving in the sea, her blindness was not what she feared. What she worried about was whether she would find an instructor willing to work with her. Here is the delightful story of her adventure:

Jacques Cousteau, the French oceanographer and inventor of the aqualung, has always been a hero of mine. When I was a kid, I used to dive vicariously by watching him on television. The fish and other sea life brought to me by his camera fascinated me.

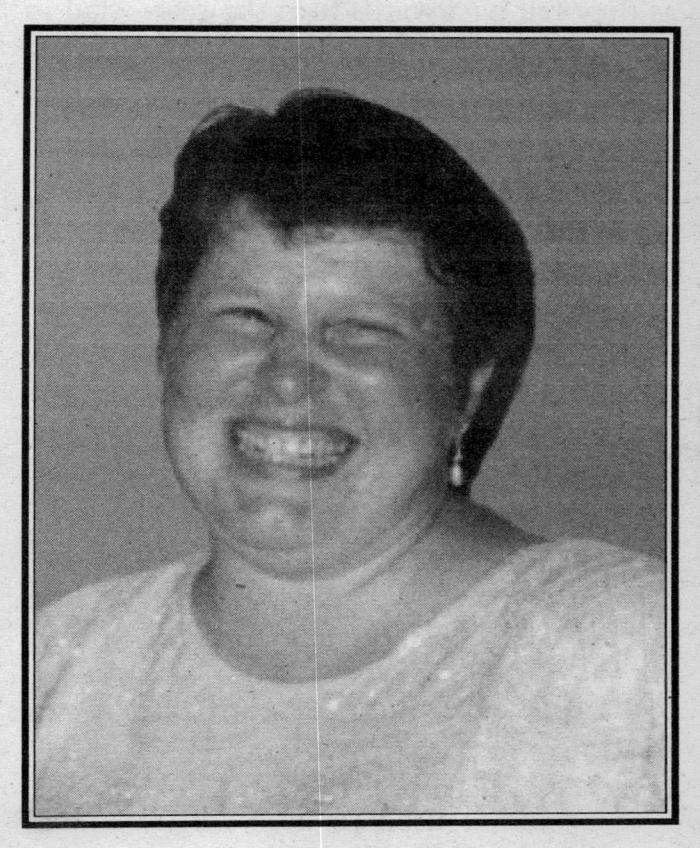

Terri Uttermohlen

I also admired the younger French divers as they fell backwards into the sea—clad in wet suits, masks, fins, and tanks. It seemed like magic to me to be able to enter another world so close, and yet so different, from the one inhabited by those of us dependent on air for our survival.

It may not surprise you then to find that I wanted to try diving on a recent trip to a small island in the Caribbean on my belated honeymoon. My husband Jim and I planned the trip for months. Though we had both traveled out of the country several times before, it would be our first trip alone together. Jim and I are blind, a circumstance that led us to some unusual speculation about how we would be received and what techniques we would use to maximize the freedom and pleasure we would have on our trip.

After much Internet research, planning, shopping, and contemplation we still had many questions as we took off from the

Madison, Wisconsin, airport: Would our inadequate French be enough to help us get around? Should we carry our canes in the water the first time we went in? Did we have enough money for all of the shopping and fine dining we were hoping to do? Would dive shops freak out at the idea of a blind person wanting to dive in the sea?

We had been on the island for two days when I ran into Sebastian, a small man from Paris who ran the activities desk at our hotel.

"Is there any way I can help you with water sports?" he asked us after pointing out a bench for us to rest upon while waiting for our tour guide.

"I would like to scuba dive," I said boldly, anticipating an argument.

Instead he responded surprised, but willing, "I can help you arrange that."

Reassured that this dream might be realized I told him that I would call the dive shop later to set something up.

On Tuesday I stood nervously in front of the activities desk wearing a sarong, my swimsuit, a hat, and enough sunscreen to grease a car. My transportation to the dive shop arrived, and we were introduced.

Mark, my instructor, drove us across the island, over a steep, poorly graded road to the hotel that housed the dive shop. We conversed a little on the way. His English was fairly good, and he seemed only a little nervous about my blindness.

When we arrived at the pool, Mark showed me the fins, mask, regulator, and tank. He was a good instructor and explained step by step what he wanted me to do. He held my hand and said I should squeeze his hand twice if I was having a problem and once if I was OK. He taught me how to inflate my tank vest using a valve to control buoyancy.

The first time into the pool, he had me simply place my face in the water and breathe through the regulator. Since I made it around the pool a couple of times successfully doing that, he guided me deeper and deeper until we touched the bottom of the pool.

Finally, he asked me to sit on the bottom. My only challenge was, being well blessed by Mother Nature and an abundance of fine Wisconsin cheese in my diet, I had trouble swimming below the surface. Some weights solved that problem, and I soon sat cross-legged on the bottom until Mark signaled me to rise.

The lesson over, Mark said that we could dive the next afternoon in the sea. I was pleased to have passed the test, and even more pleased that he had relaxed considerably with me.

The next afternoon, I stood on the warm boards of the marina, trying to squeeze my ample Midwestern flesh into a wetsuit. I succeeded in stuffing myself into my new skin and handed Mark all of my land clothes for safekeeping.

I reached for my cane and discovered it had taken a walk with a curious eight-year-old son of the dive shop owner while I was occupied with the wetsuit. It was quickly retrieved.

Finally equipped for my adventure, I clambered into the boat.

The tropical sun beat upon me as I rested on the bench at the back of the boat. I was the only American on board. As the dive boat moved into the harbor, its roundly inflated sides pulsing with the impact of the waves, I sat and listened to the French-speaking voices around me. Was I really there? I felt like I had been transported into the Jacques Cousteau films I used to watch.

I sat hoping that I would enter the water before the commercial break.

The ride to the dive spot was brief. Mark and I waited on the boat while the other divers and their instructor made their respective splashes into and under the waves. While I waited my turn, I let the French conversation between Mark and the mother of a particularly young diver pour over me like sun-warmed wine. I could understand only a bit and instead focused my drowsy mind on imagining the scene around me.

Eventually the others returned, and I donned the fins, re-zipped the sausage wrapping, put the mask on, and daintily jumped off the side of the boat into the warm Caribbean. Mark swam to me and helped me put on the tank and the weights.

Because of the wetsuit, the weights had to be very tight on me before they would stay where they were intended. The first attempt had them sliding almost immediately to encircle my thighs. Since I had no aspiration to emulate the swimming style of a mermaid, I suggested that we try again. After much giggling on my part, we finally put them successfully around my waist.

Being cautious, Mark repeated the exercise of the pool. First we swam around the boat with my face in the water, making sure I was comfortable breathing through the regulator. I reassured Mark several times by squeezing his hand once in response to his questioning squeeze that I was OK. I was far better than OK, but we hadn't worked out a signal for "wow!!!" Eventually we began to descend in the water.

My first impression of the dive was Mark's reassuring hand in mine, the bubble of my breath rising from around my face, and the sun-warmed water surrounding me.

We slowly descended to the bottom. As we swam, I ran my hands along the surface of the coarse sand of shell fragments. I hoped that Mark would warn me if I were about to grab one of the Caribbean's less friendly residents.

As we swam, Mark would tap my right arm when he wanted to guide my hand to show me things. I touched rocks bearded with algae, a tiny closed clam, and a conch shell that I believe still encased the conch. I saw sea plants that looked like firmly planted garden weeds and beautiful slime-oozing strands of tall sponges shaped like kielbasa.

Mark placed my hands on coral, stubby sponges, and sea fans. One type of sea fan made of fuzzy finger-wide tendrils seemed to pull itself away from my touch. Another type had wide rigid leaves that didn't move at all.

I was amazed when I touched coral. This variety was a hard globe with a pattern of lines and swirls incised into the surface. After touching the coral, my arm began to burn. I pointed to it, but of course Mark was unable to explain that it was Fire Coral at the time. Instead, he squeezed my hand to ask, "Are you all right?" Since the burning was minor, I squeezed back reassurance, and we swam on.

Finally, I could hear that the tank was emptying of air. My throat was dry from the regulator, and I knew my time under the sea was almost over. Mark gave the signal, and we arose.

On the surface of the water Mark told me that he had been surprised a moment before by a three-foot-long Great Barracuda. The fish barely noticed us and swam peaceably around ten meters from us. Mark had forgotten that I wouldn't see it and was momentarily afraid that I would panic. Had I sensed fear from him, I might have been afraid, but my trust, by then, was absolute.

We swam back the short distance to the boat. Mark removed my tank, and he handed it and my weights to the other instructor. I handed up my goggles and asked if I should remove the fins. Mark responded, as you like.

Next came the least graceful moment of the excursion. As I recounted earlier, I was stuffed into the wetsuit. The boat was round, rubber, wet, and about four feet above the water. There was no ladder or rope to hold onto. In younger days, it would have been relatively easy to pull myself up onto the boat. These are not my younger days, however, and years of heavy computer use have left my hands and arms weak.

I reached my arms above to grasp the upper side of the boat. Helpful hands pulled on me like a Thanksgiving wishbone. Mark pushed from below. I was laughing and out of breath, so I could not explain that the men pulling on my arms were making it impossible for me to help myself get into the boat. After much pulling, pushing, squealing, and laughter on the part of the slim Europeans who surrounded me, I was finally able to say, "Let me try." Thus I finally flopped aboard, relieved and a little embarrassed.

As we made the short bouncy trip back to the marina, Mark handed me a small beautiful snail shell. Of all of the shells I had examined when diving, this was the most perfectly formed. He presented it to me as a keepsake.

I inquired to make sure that no one was occupying the shell. I didn't like the idea of evicting a small creature from the water. Nor did I relish the possibility of that same creature emerging into my hand to register its complaint at the rude treatment.

I could not express my thanks to Mark for understanding and respecting my desire to experience the sea. He said that he really enjoyed the experience.

After we arrived at the dock, Mark helped me peel off the wetsuit. (Without his aid I would have needed a shoehorn and about a quart of WD-40.) I threw my clothes on over my swim gear, and we drove back to my hotel.

When I returned, I found Jim contentedly sunning himself on the beach. The rest of our honeymoon trip was wonderful, romantic, and sun-filled. We arrived home after an endless day of cancelled flights and plane malfunctions. As soon as we arrived, we unpacked to ensure that everything had traveled safely.

In the bottom of one of the suitcases I found the perfectly formed, delicate, gray and white shell. I marveled at the beauty of the shell and the fact that I had finally lived that long-held dream of being under the sea.

Thank you Jacques. Now you are even more my hero.

You can help us spread the word...

...about our Braille Readers Are Leaders contest for blind schoolchildren, a project which encourages blind children to achieve literacy through Braille.

...about our scholarships for deserving blind college students.

...about Job Opportunities for the Blind, a program that matches capable blind people with employers who need their skills.

...about where to turn for accurate information about blindness and the abilities of the blind.

Most importantly, you can help us by sharing what you've learned about blindness in these pages with your family and friends. If you know anyone who needs assistance with the problems of blindness, please write:

Marc Maurer, President
National Federation of the Blind
1800 Johnson Street, Suite 300
Baltimore, Maryland 21230-4998

Other Ways You Can Help the National Federation of the Blind

Write to us for tax-saving information on bequests and planned giving programs.

OR

Include the following language in your will:

"I give, devise, and bequeath unto National Federation of the Blind, 1800 Johnson Street, Suite 300, Baltimore, Maryland 21230, a District of Columbia nonprofit corporation, the sum of $_____ (or "___ percent of my net estate" or "The following stocks and bonds:_____") to be used for its worthy purposes on behalf of blind persons."

Your Contributions Are Tax-deductible